A Hidden Gift

Lessons Learned when Obstacles Become Blessings

Suzy Augustin

A Hidden Gift
Lessons Learned when Obstacles become blessings
by Suzy Augustin

Printed in the United States of America

ISBN 9781624193200

www.xulonpress.com

Testimonials

A beautiful story of love, courage and perseverance against all odds.

A Hidden Gift will make you laugh, cry and cheer out loud.

First time author, Suzy Augustin, takes you through the trials, triumphs and rewards of raising a child with special needs. Walk with Michael as he faces everyday life challenges with a mother who refused to accept no for an answer.

Intertwined within the story, you'll discover creative ways the author dealt with everyday fears and struggles.

A must read for all parents, educators and people who believe that ALL children are special and can beat the odds.

Adrienne C. Reynolds

Coral Springs, FL

Suzy's book is not only true, but very inspirational and life changing.

Her family and son have faced many challenges, tears and obstacles, but they have been persistent and continued with a positive upbeat outlook. Today, their son is able to read, write, use an iPhone, and even ride a bike. It is only because of the love, hard work and encouragement that their family has given him that he is able to do these things.

I highly encourage anyone who needs a lift to read Suzy›s book! It is funny, encouraging and captivating. It opens our eyes to what families of children with special needs have to go through on a daily basis.

Hats off to the people of the world like Suzy and her family who are able to make lemonade out of lemons! Refreshing!

Kathleen DuPont

Davie, FL

This book is a great and evolving story that keeps the reader interested and inspired. It takes you on a very personal journey where you get to experience the pain, the trials and the triumphs of this mother and her son. You will feel the frustrations that are involved when raising a special needs child, as well as the joys of every minute victory. It is a concise, poignant and motivating narrative that will not disappoint.

Mariane Augustin
Plantation, FL

Moving!!! Inspirational!!! I thoroughly enjoyed this book! The power of love is beautifully displayed throughout its chapters. You don't have to have a handicapped child to appreciate the message of this book -- and that is that we can rise above life's challenges through hard work, persistence and faith!

Alicia Mason
Brooklyn, NY

I am elated that Suzy decided to put this book together. Now, everyone who reads it will have an opportunity to experience the inspiring story of Michael's and Suzy's journey. The journey that for many years has left me in awe of her determination and perseverance in improving Mike's quality of life. This story will not only inspire you, as it has for me for many years, to truly appreciate the things we often take for granted. Mike's life journey has been "A Hidden Gift" for many.

Lissette Read
Davie, Florida

Acknowledgements

To God: Thank you for letting me see what I couldn't see on my own.

To my husband: Thank you for working so hard to provide the opportunity and support for me to do what I needed to do to help Michael.

To my family and friends: Thank you for your support; without it, I would have lost my sanity.

"Never give up" and "I'm not going down." Those are the phrases I live by when my son becomes aggressive, when he pulls my hair, throws things, or digs his nails into my skin because he wants me to stop challenging him or avoid the work he has to do. I say to him, "Someone is going down and it's not going to be me." It doesn't matter if he's handicapped; he has to learn to behave appropriately and my job is to teach him how to do that. I would rather him fight with me -- his mother -- and would rather struggle to teach him to do the right thing than to have him hurt someone else.

My book is a story that I think everyone can relate to, feel good about, and hopefully be motivated and become inspired by. It doesn't matter if you're young, old, a parent with a special needs child or with normal children. We all go through trials, obstacles and pain. It's part of life.

I wrote this book to provide encouragement and show strength, not to make people sad. I want to emphasize: Never give up, no matter what!! The situation may seem grim or depressing at the time and it will be. But if you hang in there and allow yourself to grow, learn and not fight it, you will emerge a much stronger and better person for it.

Contents

Part 1

Prologue

S ome people say each person has their own personal, unique story. You know what I've realized is that we don't; our stories are basically the same. What we have is the same story, but different parts or roles that we are given. Some people are given similar roles or situations. This is why we can relate to each other's stories. When we say our story is unique, I think in some ways (subconsciously) we are devaluing the other person's situation. Are we saying that I'm so special and so important that I was given a unique story or my story is much more important than yours? Everyone shares or will feel the pain of a lost loved one, feelings of hurt so bad that it caused thoughts of suicide, and we all have asked these questions: "Why me, God?" and "Why am I here?"

For me the question "Why me, God?" was answered one day while walking in the halls on my way back to my classroom. As an early childhood school teacher, I am always thinking about what I can do to help my students learn better or what I can do to help them understand a particular method or concept. You must remember I work with 5 to 7 year olds. Most of the time, I use their favorite television show as an example in order to bring the point home. This particular day, I remember asking myself the question while walking back to the classroom, "God, why give me a handicapped child? I'm a good person, I have not killed 20 people, and I try to do the right thing." Suddenly, I heard an answer from deep inside. The answer was three simple words: "WHY NOT YOU?" I don't know if it was what you would call an epiphany but, at that moment, I understood everything (almost). You see, I thought I was better than the next person. I was saying that God should burden or punish someone else with a disabled child, someone less worthy, someone less important or valuable. God said to me that day, "You are not more valuable or worthy than my other children; you are the same." Suddenly, I felt an overwhelming sense of humility and shame, and I wanted to drop to my knees and beg God for his forgiveness.

Chapter 1

Michael's Birth

After living and teaching in south Florida for three years, I was working on my teaching certificate and trying to get credit for my teaching experiences from New York transferred to Miami-Dade County Public Schools.

Four years after I had Brittany, a beautiful little girl, Michael was born. The pregnancy was uneventful. I went to work every day and I was not sick and didn't have any morning sickness. I enjoyed being pregnant. I ate everything and a lot of it. I think I gained 50 to 60 pounds, starting from 100 pounds at the beginning of my pregnancy. I think being pregnant was my opportunity to eat whatever I wanted without feeling guilty. I think I ate an ice cream cake each week until I delivered. Thinking back, boy was I big!

My Florida teaching certificate finally came in, so I decided to drive personally to the Miami-Dade school board downtown office. At five months pregnant, I felt great. School was out for the summer and I really had nothing to do. It was the month of July and a nice sunny day as I traveled the 45 minutes drive downtown. I thought driving there and bringing the certificate myself would expedite the process of moving me from a substitute teacher to a full–time, certified teacher. I was excited and couldn't wait to change my status to a real teacher. That day I left my daughter with my mother, thinking I would be able to move faster and get errands done without having to entertain a four-year-old. I got into my little Nissan Sentra, put on my seat belt and drove to downtown Miami. I parked the car in a paid parking lot and went inside the office.

Once inside, it took me a very short time to take care what I needed. I took the same road I always take coming from downtown. There was nothing different about that particular street, except the traffic light was not working. So I decided to slow down before entering the highway. I don't know how it happened or when the other car actually hit me, but I lost control and crashed head on into the street light pole.

I got out of the car feeling fine. I didn't even realize that the car was completely smashed and had become part of the pole. I don't know how I made it out without any physical damage.

Then I started thinking about the baby. I immediately swallowed hard to see if it would move. I didn't feel anything. I don't remember how the police got there or who called. The officer asked me if I wanted to go to the hospital, and I said I wanted to wait for my husband to take me. We called the tow truck for the car and my husband and I went to the hospital and into the emergency room. They gave me a sonogram to see if the baby was all right. That was the day I found out that the baby was going to be a boy. After the sonogram, they told me everything looked fine.

Two weeks after the accident, I started having early contractions. My contractions were coming every hour. At five months pregnant, I was put on bed rest for the remainder of the pregnancy and was given medication to stop or slow down the contractions. I had to stay hydrated and in bed. I could only get up for a shower and to go to the bathroom. During the three months I was on bed rest, I never prayed so hard in my life. One day, I was so desperate to make sure that the baby was going to be all right; I even called one of the Christian shows on the Trinity Broadcast television station and asked them if they could pray with me on the phone. I figured I would try anything and everything. I visited the doctor every three weeks. Eventually, I went every week until the contractions started coming from every hour down to every 15 minutes. I delivered Michael at 38 weeks by C-section. He weighed 6 pounds 8 ounces. This delivery, I felt, was more difficult than my first. I felt different and took longer to recover than with my daughter's delivery. It seems that after I had my daughter, I was up and felt better faster.

Everything seemed fine in the hospital. The baby was a little jaundiced, but I was told everything looked fine. I took Michael home a few days later. He seemed to want to eat every 45 minutes. I was breast feeding at the time, and it looked like he was not getting full or did not want to last the recommended two to three hour wait between feeding. I started feeding on demand, but that took a toll on me. I breast fed for about two months and then started the bottle. After one month, Michael had put on 10 pounds and I also noticed his right eye was constantly producing mucus and would not open completely, while the other eye looked fine and alert.

By his second month, he was close to 20 pounds. He looked huge to me. However, the doctors didn't seem concerned about the weight gain. At the same time, the right eye was continuing to produce mucus and was not opening. When I mentioned this to the doctor, he told me that sometimes that happens to babies and eventually the eye would open and be fine. He gave me medication to apply to the eye. When the right eye finally opened, I sensed something odd about it. I also noticed the way he kept his head. When I picked him up, he kept his head tilted to one side.

One afternoon, I was sitting in my husband's office and holding Michael. While looking at his face, I noticed the pupil in the right eye was very small while the pupil in the left eye was large. I got up and went outside in the light and the right pupil never changed. However, the left pupil got small. I decided to turn the lights on and off to check the pupils. I

23

felt this odd sensation in the pit of my stomach and I knew this wasn't good. I immediately called the doctor and he told me to come to the office first thing in morning. When I got to the office, the nurse sent me right in.

The doctor examined Michael's eye again and told me that, based on the quick weight gain and his pupil not being able to dilate, he thought my son might have a brain tumor. When he said those words, I don't know if I went into shock, but there was numbness all over my body. The doctor looked nervous. I just wanted to know what was wrong with Michael. The doctor immediately called Children's Hospital and set up an MRI.

The MRI showed some brain injury. He suffered most of the injury on the right side of his brain. This caused damage to the section of the brain that handles speech, coordination, fine and gross motor skills. The brain injury also caused cerebral palsy (CP), and torticollis. The CP causes weakness to the entire right side of his body. He doesn't have function of his right arm or hand and, when walking, he drags his right foot. Torticollis is weakness of the muscles of the neck. As a result, he keeps his head tilted to the right. This will eventually cause the head and face to appear out of shape.

I was also told to visit a pediatric ophthalmologist, an eye specialist, to find out what was going on with his eye. After a full examination of Michael's eyes, he was diagnosed with optic nerve atrophy in his right eye and perfect vision in his left. The ophthalmologist described it as a camera with no film. In other words, the eye physically looked normal, but was missing certain parts in order to function. The doctor also said that it's possible the accident may have stopped or interrupted the development of the tissues around the right eye. As I listened to the doctor's analogy and diagnosis, I didn't quite understand the depth and fullness of my situation. I just listened. However, the full comprehension and understanding would come later.

Chapter 2

A Miracle at Wal-Mart

It was just an ordinary day like any other -- running errands and walking out of Wal-Mart with my 10-year-old daughter, pushing Michael in his stroller. On my way to the car, a well–dressed, middle-aged woman stopped me and said, "I remember you and your son." At first I was cautious and not sure what she was talking about because I didn't remember her. I continued to talk because I didn't want to appear rude. However, I was wary of her and on my guard. She said, "I remember talking to you last year in Wal-Mart. I have been praying for you ever since."

After that statement, I thought this woman was completely out of her mind because I didn't remember talking to her. The woman continued to speak. She said, "Have you decided on a school yet or are you home schooling your son?"

All this time, I thought she had the wrong person in mind. But she continued. She said, "You told me that you were not happy with the school system and you were not sure what you were going to do. I want you to know that your son looks great and God wants you to know that you are doing a great job. That day when I met you, I started praying for you."

Now I was on the verge of tears. I didn't want her to see me cry, so I nodded my head and walked quickly to my car. Once in my car, I burst out crying -- and I mean sobbing. I looked into my daughter's face and she looked confused. I explained to my daughter why I was crying. I said, "You can look at this situation two ways. One, this woman was talking to the wrong person and made a mistake or, two, somehow God spoke through her to tell me not to worry and that I am doing a good job with my son and to continue being strong."

I felt nobody understood what I was going through. My husband was having a difficult time coping. He broke down every time he looked at Michael. My husband is a very good man and I know this was not the time to place blame or get upset because he was not ready to handle or accept the situation. I knew it was up to me to prepare Michael for him, to teach Michael a way to communicate with his father and maybe his father wouldn't be so nervous and scared around him.

My extended family wasn't quite sure how to help me, but I know they wanted to. They do help me in their own way. They take care of Michael for a couple of days so I can travel with my husband or a couple of hours, so I can have some "me" time. I am grateful to them for that. I had to be strong for my husband and help my family cope and understand, and teach them how to interact with a child that didn't talk and was physically slow. I had to set the stage on how Michael should be treated. No pity, don't spoil him. Treat him as a normal child. If he does something you don't like, tell him so. Don't be scared! I had to prepare him for the outside world. I had to carry the burden of teaching my family how to interact with my son and preparing Michael to act so that his father could feel comfortable interacting with him and not be nervous or scared.

That Wal-Mart experience gave me the strength to move on and to continue what I've been doing with Michael and not to give up, no matter what. After that point, nothing could stop me. I started reading books on brain development and behavior. That day renewed my strength; I feel I didn't need therapy or a support group. That day, I got my answer and therapy at the same time. I told my daughter that I believed this was not a coincidence. I could choose to believe that this woman made a mistake and feel miserable and be a victim and feel sorry for myself, or I could take it as a sign and move forward and deal with whatever came my way. It was a choice!

A friend once asked me if I was upset with my husband for not being able to handle the situation or support me emotionally. After thinking about it, I don't think I was ever upset with him. I saw my husband as someone who was hurt, frustrated and very angry for his son. It's not that he didn't want to help me, but he simply couldn't help. He had to come to terms with Michael's disability and accept it and he was not there yet. So, what did I do? I learned to be patient, calm and understanding. We couldn't both be a mess! So we decided that my husband would focus on his work and provide financially so I could stay home and help teach Michael and bring him to a level where he would be able to function outside his world and, at same time, allow my husband time to deal with his own anger.

I was so excited about the Wal-Mart experience that I went home and told my mother, my sister and friends and anyone who would listen. Angels do walk among us. I often wonder about that lady; my own personal angel sent from God to give me hope, strength, and assurance that I was not going to have to go through this alone.

Chapter 3

Two Short Stories that Changed My Outlook on Life

W hen I first read this short story, I had a different reaction than my friend who had a disabled son. She gave me this story to make me feel better about my situation. After reading it, I saw it differently than she did. Here is the story.

Welcome to Holland

By Emily Perl Kingsley

I am often asked to describe the experience of raising a child with a disability – to try to help people who have not shared that unique experience to understand it, to imagine how it

31

would feel, it's like this ... when you're going to have a baby, it's like planning a fabulous trip to Italy. You buy a bunch of guidebooks and make your wonderful plans. The Coliseum. Michelangelo's David. The gondolas in Venice. You may learn some handy phrases in Italian, It's all very exciting. After months of eager anticipation, the day finally arrives. You pack your bags and off you go. Several hours later, the plane lands, the stewardess comes in and say, "Welcome to Holland."

"Holland?!?" you say. "What do you mean Holland?? I signed up for Italy! I'm supposed to be in Italy! All my life I've dreamed of going to Italy." But there's been a change in the flight plan. They've landed in Holland and there you must stay. To a horrible, disgusting, filthy place, full of pestilence, famine, and disease. It's just a different place. So you must go out and buy new guidebooks. And you must learn a whole new language.

And you will meet a whole new group of people you would never have met. It's just a different place. It's slower- paced than Italy, less flashy than Italy. But after you've been there for a while and you catch your breath. You look around... and you begin to notice that Holland has windmills... and Holland has tulips. Holland even has Rembrandts. But everyone you know is busy coming and going from Italy. And they're all bragging about what a wonderful time they had there. And for the rest of your life, you will say, "Yes, that's where I was supposed to go. That's what I had planned." And the pain of that will never, ever, ever, ever go away... because the loss of that dream is a very, very significant loss. But if you spend your life mourning the fact that you didn't get to Italy, you may never be free to enjoy the very special, the very lovely things... about Holland.

I know that this story might help many people understand or have some idea of how it would feel to have a disabled child. But when I read the story, I said to myself, "How sad for this woman who wanted something perfect, and nothing is perfect."

I thought about a young woman who dreams about marrying a rich man and having everything she ever wanted, because all her life she hears people say how wonderful it was to be rich and have lots money and houses. But she marries a poor man who works hard and is a good person, and now she feels bad that she didn't marry a rich man and is stuck with a poor man. Because of that, she doesn't appreciate what she has and how wonderful he is.

When I had my son, I thought to myself, *This is what I got and this is fine and I going to love him just the way he is and help him be the best person he can be. I'm not going to feel sorry about something that I wish I had or bury something that I never had.*

The following is a short story by author Erma Bombeck and it affected me profoundly.

Some Mothers are Chosen Very Carefully

By Erma Bombeck

Most women become mothers by accident, some by choice, a few by social pressures and a couple by habit. This year nearly 100,000 women will become mothers of handicapped children. Did you ever wonder how mothers of handicapped children are chosen? Somehow I visualize God hovering over Earth selecting his instruments for propagation with great care and deliberation. As he observes, he instructs his angels to make notes in a giant ledger. "Armstrong, Beth; son; patron saint, Mathew.

"Forrest, Marjorie; daughter; patron saint, Cecelia.

"Rudledge, Carrie; twins; patron saint... give her Gerard. He's used to profanity."

Finally, he passes a name to an angel and

35

smiles, "Give her a handicapped child." The angel is curious. "Why this one, God? She's so happy."

"Exactly," smiles God. "Could I give a handicapped child a mother who does not know laughter? That would be cruel."

"But has she patience?" asks, the angel.

"I don't want her to have too much patience or she will drown in a sea of self-pity and despair. Once the shock-and –resentment wears off, she'll handle it. I watched her today. She has that feeling of self and independence that is so rare and so necessary in a mother. You see, the child I'm going to give her has his own world. She has to make it live in her world and that's not going to be easy."

"But, Lord, I don't think she even believes in you."

God smiles. "No matter. I can fix that. This one is perfect. She has just enough selfishness."

The angel gasps, "Selfishness? Is that a virtue?"

God nods. "If she can't separate herself from the child occasionally, she'll never survive. Yes, there is a woman whom I will bless with a child less than perfect. She doesn't realize it yet, but she is to be envied. She will never take for granted a 'spoken word.' She will never consider a 'step' ordinary. When her child says 'Momma' for the first time, she will be present at a miracle and know it! When she describes a tree or a sunset to her blind child, she will see it as few people ever see my creations.

"I will permit her to see clearly the things I see – ignorance, cruelty, prejudice – and allow her to rise above them. She will never be alone. I will be at her side every minute of every day of her life because she is doing my work as surely as she is here by my side."

37

"And what about her patron saint?" asks

the angel, his pen poised in midair.

God smiles. "A mirror will suffice."

When I first read this short story, I cried so hard that I couldn't finish reading it. I had to read it three times in order to finish it. I was able to relate to the author's description of the last mother. I felt that she was describing me, especially when I talk to my son and the way I describe things to him. It's like I'm experiencing the ordinary in a new and glorious way. It is like a newfound appreciation and love of the simple things and everything. Sometimes, I wish I could show people what I see. How happy they would feel and how they would appreciate who they are and where they are and still rise above it.

Chapter 4

The Christmas Show

Michael's Christmas show in kindergarten brought the hammer down on my decision to take him out of school and educate him myself. I can laugh about this now, but back then, I felt frustrated and wanted to cry. I didn't want to see him in that state.

When Michael's teacher told me that the class was going to put on a Christmas show and she wanted to include Michael, my first reaction was, "Oh, noooooooo!" This was not going to be good. Since day one in kindergarten, Michael had not behaved. Every day, he would get a sad face on his daily report. Sometimes, he would spend half the day or all day in time out. How in the world was he going to cooperate with the teacher and stand still for ten to fifteen minutes performing a song? I told her that I don't think this was a good idea. But she said we would work with him and to give it a try

At that time I was living with my parents, and my mom was a great help to me and Michael. I told my mom about the show and how nervous I was. She said, "Don't worry; there's nothing you can do at this point. Just do it."

Before the show, we would practice every day at home on how to stand on a stage. I practiced with Michael on how to behave during the show. I would say to him, "Don't hit anyone. Be nice and stand still."

On the day of the show, I drove Michael to school. On the way there, I put on my happy face. We talked about having fun in the show and how proud I was of him for being a good boy and all that good stuff.

When we arrived at the school, I took Michael to his class and then went to sit in the auditorium to wait for the show. As I was sitting there, I was rubbing my hands together, taking deep breaths and pleading with God for this show to go well. I begged God, "Please, please, please don't let him hit anyone on that stage today. He can hit tomorrow, but not today."

His class was the first to perform. The class came out on the stage with Michael at the end of the line. When the class turned and faced the audience, I noticed the teacher's aide standing next to Michael and the teacher on the other end. I was kind of relieved when I saw an adult next to him. I thought, "Maybe it won't be so bad." Well, I spoke to soon. Before the song even started, Michael hit a student next to him. The aide quickly grabbed his hand and put it down. Seconds later, he did it again and again. At this point, I couldn't look any more and I left and went straight home. I didn't cry, but I felt defeated, like someone had sucked all my energy from me. I didn't know what to do.

When I got home and opened the door, I didn't even have a chance to get inside the house when my mom walked up to me and said, "Why are you back so soon?" I told her what had happened, and what Michael did. Suddenly, her facial features changed from worry to upset. I couldn't believe what she told me next. She said that I had to go back and finish watching the show and I couldn't leave like that. That's not what I wanted to hear. I didn't want of go back. Still standing at the door, I told her I would pick him up later. She continued with a firm voice, this time saying that I should go back now! I didn't argue because, in my heart, I knew she was right. I turned back and drove to the school.

When I got there, the Christmas show had just ended. The other parents were still hanging around. I walked straight into Michael's classroom and spoke to the teacher. I told her that I was sorry about what had happened.

Michael never went back after that Christmas show. I started to home school.

Chapter 5

Educating Michael
Kindergarten

WOW! Where do I start? You have to remember that Michael wore diapers until he was six years old and he was still using a walker to walk. Because of the CP, he used a walker from the age of eight months until he was six years old. With extensive physical therapy seven days a week, two hours a day, he was able to stop using the walker and move on his own. That means I continued physical therapy at home, long after the therapist left. He was non-verbal, but he could hear, which caused major frustration. By the time Michael was ready for kindergarten, he was functioning at a level between 12 and 24 months of age.

I was afraid for my son. I was thinking like a teacher, *This kid is not ready for anything, let alone school.* He was angry all the time, very aggressive. He would pull my hair, scratch my arms, and bite me. I was frustrated with him all the time. He would throw chairs and pull my clothes. When he got angry, he would grab anything that was near to throw at me. I still have my battle scars. I started to call him Lucifer or Damian. Damian was from an old movie about a little evil boy who happens to be the son of Satan. I was thinking, *How is he going to function in a place where you have to follow rules and listen to the teacher?* He wasn't even listening to me and he seemed like he didn't even care. I didn't want to send him to a place where I knew he wasn't going to be successful and get frustrated. However, I had no choice and decided to enroll Michael in kindergarten.

At that time my husband, started a business and I had to go back to work. Financially, my husband and I were struggling. We sold our home and moved in with my parents. We lived with my parents for seven years while my husband was trying to build his business. Those years were very difficult for our marriage.

My husband was in denial for a long time. He kept saying, "Michael will be all right. He's going to talk and he will

44

be fine." I knew if I didn't find a way to help him with his aggression and behavior, one day he would hurt or kill someone and they wouldn't care if he was disabled. He would either end up in a mental institution or jail, and I could not let that happen.

One week before school started, I attended a kindergarten orientation for parents. That's when you meet your child's teacher and other parents. During the orientation, I was watching the other children with their parents and the principal talking about all the wonderful and exciting activities the children would be doing in class. All I was thinking was, *These people are not talking about my son because my son can't do any of these things. They don't know what is in store for them.*

I looked at the children and their interaction with each other, playing and doing kid's stuff and I was thinking, *Oh my God. These kids will not play with my son, but will be afraid of him and make fun of him. He is not ready to be a part of this.* Even though I was frustrated, It didn't last long. I knew I couldn't just stop and do nothing, so I didn't dwell

45

on my problem or think how bad it was for long. I just knew I had to move forward and do something.

The first day of school, I took Michael to school and waited with him. I wanted to talk to the teacher and let her know about his behavior. I told her, "My son can become very aggressive because he is non-verbal. He will hit and bite if he tries to communicate and you don't understand." She told me not to worry and that she had experience with students like Michael. She saw that I was worried and tried to assure me that everything was going to be all right. I kissed Michael, told him to behave and left for work. All day at work, I was thinking about how his day was going. I couldn't wait to pick him up.

On the way to pick up Michael, I prayed, "Please God, let him have a good day." I kept saying those words over and over until I got to the school. When I got to the school, I saw him in front of his walker, standing with the aide. Michael was in a special class with about 8 students and two aides. The aide brought him to my car and I asked, "How was Michael?"

She said, "He was all right; there's a note in his book bag."

I thought, *Oh, my God! He's got a note!*

Once in the car, I asked Michael how his day was. You have to remember, Michael doesn't talk. He would nod or shake his head for yes or no when you asked him questions and that was it. If he wanted something, he would bring it to you or show you what he wanted. Sometimes, if I couldn't figure out what he wanted, he would throw something, break something or hit me. So when I asked him about his day, he didn't answer, he just turned his face and ignored me. I knew his day was bad

I opened the book bag and took out his folder. In the folder was a form that showed what he did and his behavior during each activity. During reading, he hit the teacher when she walked by him and he pulled a little girl's hair during recess. He was sent to time out. His aggressive behavior continued over several weeks. I sent a note to the teacher about bringing in the school behaviorist as soon as possible because I didn't want him to hurt another child. The school tried several strategies, but nothing worked. Michael was spending half the day or more in time out in the classroom.

I was getting frustrated with the school and tired of bad notes being sent home about his behavior. I became nervous and dreaded 2:00pm when I had to pick him up from school, because I knew what I would hear. Even the students in his class would tell me that Michael hit them or pulled their hair before I read the note. By this time, Michael had been in kindergarten for four months. I talked to my husband about taking a leave of absence from my job and home schooling Michael. Before deciding to take him out of school, I spoke to his teacher. I told her that if the school couldn't help me with my son, then I was going to have to take him out and home school him myself.

After the Christmas recess, Michael did not return to school. I spent two weeks during the Christmas break thinking and planning how to educate a disabled, non verbal, and functioning at 24 months old child. I thought, *Since I'm a teacher of regular kids, all I have to do is bring my lesson plan a couple of notches down to his level. How difficult can it be?* I felt positive and optimistic about doing this. By this time, we were still living with my parents and my husband's business was still not going well. So my husband and I decided that I would stay home and work with Michael and he would get another job.

I got permission from my father to turn his den into a classroom for Michael. I waited and started home schooling Michael the day that all the other students went back to school after the New Year. In the morning, my daughter got ready to leave for her school and I prepared my son for his school. By this time, my daughter Brittany was 10 years old. From day one, I explained to Brittany, my niece and nephews what happened to Michael. I made sure to treat Michael like any other child and I wanted them to do the same and not feel sorry for him or pity him. I wanted them to talk and play with him as much as they could. If Michael did something wrong or hit one of them, they were to tell me. He would be punished, just like any other kid.

The day was planned as a regular school day. We said the pledge, did the morning announcements, and we had recess. My goal was to teach him and prepare him for a time when he would be able to return to school. Instead of a whole classroom full of students, I had one.

As a teacher, I put my skills to work. I found a great book that helped me plan for a child like Michael. The book was called *One-on-One: Working with Low-Functioning Children with Autism and Other Developmental Disabilities* by Marilyn Chassman. I used this book like the Bible. It provided resources and lessons that I could adjust to fit my child's needs. I prepared myself as if I was going to teach a regular toddler. I got pencils, paper, crayons -- everything you would need to teach reading writing and math. We started with the letter A. I handed Michael a pencil to trace the letter. He couldn't even hold the pencil. When I tried to hold his hand to help him trace the letter, he bit me and ripped up the paper. I told him, "You're going to do this!" I put another piece of paper down, held his hand and forced him to trace it. This went on for about 10 minutes. Every time I put a paper down, he would rip it or attempt to hit me. I told Michael, "You are not going to make me stop. You can do this!"

This situation went on for a couple of days. After a week, Michael came up with a new strategy to get out of work.

Once we would start working, he would literally fall asleep. He would sleep for three hours at his desk. This went on for months. At first, he would sleep for three hours and I would wait for him to get up. Once he got up, we continued where we left off. I wanted to show him that I wasn't going anywhere. No matter what, the work would still be there. The next month, he slept about two hours. As soon as he got up, I would still be sitting there waiting for him and we would finish the work. I told him I wasn't going anywhere and that it would be easier and quicker for him to do the work. Whether he understood me or not, he realized that he wasn't going to make me stop or get out of doing the work. By the third month he was sleeping for 30 minutes to an hour. He was still aggressive and tried to get out of doing the work, but he wasn't sleeping for hours anymore.

By this time, I was working with Michael seven days a week, three to four hours a day. I had to work with him every day, because an activity that should take one minute to complete took 30 minutes to finish. I don't know where I got the strength, but I had adopted a phrase from my principal at school and made it my own. I kept saying to myself, "FAIL-URE IS NOT AN OPTION."

I kept the three to four hour schedule with Michael all year round, holidays, summer, rain or shine. I did not stop. After the end of that year, I was able to test Michael academically. Mentally, he was functioning at a 4-year-old level. Remember, he was about 6 years old. Within that one year, Michael made great progress. Now he was able to trace lines, trace letters on his own and knew 18 letters of the alphabet and their sounds. I felt like the teacher from the book, *The Story of My Life* by Helen Keller. It is a book about a blind, deaf and mute girl that no one thought could learn. But her teacher proved them wrong. Helen Keller went on to become a famous writer and poet, so I knew there was hope for Michael.

Character cannot be developed in ease and quiet. Only through experience of trial and suffering can the soul be strengthened, ambition inspired, and success achieved.

-- Helen Keller

I wanted to make home schooling feel more like school for Michael and to create a school environment, so I decided to ask my older brother if I could include his four-year–old daughter, Chloe, in my class with Michael. Every morning, I would pick Chloe up and bring her to my house for school. I felt that with my niece, he would be interacting with a typical child on a daily basis. He would also learn appropriate behavior from her. I had classroom rules that they had to follow, activities, lunch and recess. We went to the library once a week for story time and to work on the computers. It was a funny situation at the library during story time because Michael was the biggest kid there. Story time was usually early in the day in the library and the children that were sitting around and listening to the story were mostly toddlers. No one asked questions, but some of the children stared at Michael sometimes. They were probably wondering "Why is he here?" Nevertheless, Michael, Chloe and I were there every week.

Most of the time, I had to sit behind Michael, hold him down and force him to listen to the story. His attention span was about 10 to 15 minutes and story time was 30 minutes long. Looking back now, some of our best memories were made while educating Michael.

I remember a funny story about my niece Chloe and Michael during a lesson at home. I was reviewing the letters with them, and when it was Michael's turn to answer, he didn't remember the letter, so my niece whispered the answer to him. She covered the side of her mouth and whispered the letter right into his ear. She did it as if she thought I wouldn't see her, and then Michael signed the letter. I laughed and told her that it was nice of her to help Michael, but he had to say it for himself. Sometimes she would say that she and Michael were the most popular kids in school. I would giggle and say, "Yes, you are!"

It was nice having Chloe with Michael during the last three months of the year. She played with him and talked to him like he was just a regular kid. She tried to bring him into her world and, every now and then, I believe he would get a glimpse.

Many persons have the wrong idea of what constitutes true happiness. It is not attained through self gratification, but through fidelity to a worthy purpose.

-- Helen Keller

Chapter 6

Working with the Behaviorist and Therapist

When Michael was seven, he was still in diapers and still aggressive. I enrolled him in a speech program that his therapist recommended. Nova University had just started a special program that focused on improving speech in disabled children called The Learning Center (TLC). All of the teachers there were speech therapist interns. During the four-hour program -- Monday through Thursday -- besides working on speech, they would teach the children how to use simple augmentative devices. An augmentative device is an alternative way of communication to help students and adults with language disorders use expressive language or receptive language. This can be accomplished through assistive technology devices such as computers or hand-held devices. The students were also given occupational therapy and physical therapy.

Since Michael was in this program, dealing with teachers and students, I decided to get professional help for his behavior. My husband and I made sacrifices in order to pay for private speech therapy, the speech program and a behaviorist. After the behaviorist assessed Michael, she told me that if we wanted to decrease his aggression, we would have to find a way for him to communicate better. She said Michael was very bright; receptively he seemed to understand everything. She suggested I learn sign language, so I decided to take sign languages classes at the League of Hard of Hearing Center in the evenings. The classes there were cheaper than the community college.

When I got home after each class, I would work with Michael and teach him all of the words I had learned. He was eating it up. He was absorbing this type of communication like a sponge. I wasn't learning fast enough to teach him. I think with sign language he was able to keep up with the speed of his thoughts. Due to his brain injury, only his left side of his body functioned well. He was using only his left hand to sign. Since he did not have 100% movement in his fingers, I had to modify the signs for him. The behaviorist also suggested that Michael needed more therapy to improve his walking and eating.

I decided to hire an occupational therapist that was working at the learning center with Michael. Her name was Yira Aurilia. I believe God put this woman in my path to help me. She visited Michael twice a week for an hour. Under her care, Michael improved tremendously. She not only helped his fine motor skills -- like handwriting, eating, and self help -- she also worked on gross motor skills. We took Michael to the park and worked on coordination and balance. She worked on the balance beam and taught Michael how to climb and go down the slide. She would show me how to massage and stretch his fingers and legs. I would do these stretches and pulls every day, two to three times a day. Sometimes I was so exhausted at the end of the day, I wondered who needed the therapy more – Michael or me.

Chapter 7

A Day in the Park

I remember a funny story about a day in the park with Michael. Well, I can laugh about it now but, at the time, I didn't think it was funny. Yira, the occupational therapist, decided that it would be a good idea to have therapy with Michael at the park. She thought teaching Michael how to go up and down the slide, cross the play bridge and swing on the swings would help him with his gross motor skills. We went to the park every Saturday for a month. Michael really enjoyed it and I was happy.

One day, I took Michael to the park by myself. He was about seven years old. In this particular park, they used sand in all the play areas. While playing, I had to help Michael physically go up and down the slide, help him sit on the swing and help him climb up and down the pole. We were there about an hour and I was tired. I told Michael that it was time to go home. I saw that face that he makes when he doesn't want to do something. When Michael doesn't want to do something, he usually drops to the floor, puts his head down and ignores you. At seven years old, Michael weighed about 70 pounds and I was 100 pounds. He was a big kid. He is very stubborn and I know that, when he gets like that, talking to him doesn't work.

I knew I couldn't pick him up, so I decided to drag him out. I put one of my hands under his arm and the other around his chest just like a hook and started to pull. When I started pulling him, he dropped his body more. It felt like dead weight and he had dug his heels into the sand. I was pulling him and dragging the sand with me. By the time I reached the van in the parking lot, you could see the tracks from his sneakers all the way to the car. Now that I had made it to the van, how was I going to get him inside the car?

He was still not moving and his head was down and ignoring me. I looked around and saw some people staring, but no one offered to help. I opened the door and, with a quick move, I picked him up and dumped him in the back seat. I tried to make him sit properly on the seat, but he kept his body very stiff. He looked like an ironing board left partially open. Eventually, he dropped himself on the car floor in the ironing board position. He stayed in that position until we got home.

When we finally got to the house, I pulled into the driveway, opened the doors, and he refused to get out of the car. He remained in the car with the doors open for two hours. I remembered the behavior therapist telling me to ignore him when he behaves like that. She said, "He is seeking attention." So I decided to leave him alone, but I kept sneaking around the car to see if he was okay. The behaviorist also said, "Check on him, but don't let him see you because if he sees you then he is getting the attention he seeks."

I thought, "My God! My neighbors must think I'm a crazy lady, sneaking around my car like that." At one point, he fell asleep in the van.

After two hours, he got out of the van, walked inside the house into his room, climbed into to bed and went to sleep by himself. No dinner that night!

The next time we went to the park, he behaved beautifully – lesson learned.

Chapter 8

Potty Training Michael

How do you potty train a seven-year-old? All I have to say is "OH, MY GOD!"

I told the behaviorist that I wanted to potty train Michael and if I decided to send him back to public school, I didn't want him to wear a diaper. She said that she had a program that we should try that is used with handicapped children. She gave me an article to read about the procedure.

The behaviorist told me to buy a timer. The first day we started the potty training, we only focused on getting him to urinate in the toilet. We began in the afternoon around 4 o'clock. We gave Michael some cookies and 32 ounces of juice to drink. We brought a portable TV into the bathroom, sat him on the toilet and waited. I would ask him every ten minutes if he had to pee. He would have to nod his head yes or no, and then he would get a cookie for giving me an answer and more to drink.

On the first day, he drank *a lot* of juice and I waited about 6 hours in the bathroom and he refused to go. He even took a nap while sitting on the toilet. I waited in the bathroom with him, even after the behaviorist left to go home. By ten o'clock I put a diaper on him and put him to bed.

By the next morning when he woke up, his diaper was soaked. The next day I started the process all over again. I started early in the morning. This time I didn't bring the TV in the bathroom because I wanted him to concentrate. A couple of times I tried pouring water on his penis to start the sensation of peeing. That didn't work. I tried letting the water run. No, that didn't work either. By this time we had been in the bathroom for 2 hours and he started to become aggressive.

He would point to the diaper and I would say, "No! Pee pee in the toilet!" He would get up from the toilet and hit me and throw everything he could grab from the bathroom to throw at me. I had to remove everything from the bathroom, including pictures on the wall. I would grab him and make him sit on the toilet. There was a point where I had to physically hold him down on the toilet while he was fighting to get up. I said, "Somebody's going down and it ain't gonna be me!" I even offered him ice cream -- the whole container -- if he went.

After four hours, all he'd had to eat was cookies and juice. I had never seen a kid so stubborn in all my life. By now, I was sitting on the chair, tired and looking at my son and saying to God, "Is this it? Is this the way you want it? Is this not enough punishment?"

Then that little voice came into my head, "No, It's not. Not even close." Again I kept saying, "I don't know if I can do this." With the same breath, I said, "Okay Lord, I'm ready to take whatever you dish out." I can't explain this feeling, but the more stubborn and aggressive he became, the stronger I felt.

I went to get a book to read while I waited. About an hour later, Michael stood up, faced the toilet and peed. I couldn't believe it. I hugged him, kissed him, squeezed and yelled, "You did it, you made pee pee!" I called everybody in the house to see the pee pee in the toilet. My daughter, my husband and my parents all hugged him and told him how proud they were. I called my sister and my in-laws -- I told everybody. After that, I gave him a big bowl of ice cream.

I called the behaviorist and told her what happened. She said that over the weekend I needed to buy a small timer with a clip that could be attached to his shirt or pants. I should set the timer to ring every 15 minutes and ask Michael if he had to use the bathroom. She said I should physically take him every hour. If he went within that time, I should give him praise or a treat. She also said to keep a schedule and take data on how often he was going.

On Monday morning when I brought Michael to the center, I spoke to the director of the center and told her what I was doing with Michael. She was very helpful and understanding. This time I set the timer to ring every 30 minutes and took Michael to the bathroom every hour. I said to the director, "Please make a big deal if he goes to the bathroom today and take data for me."

After that, I was no longer sending diapers but a change of clothing in case of an accident. I felt a sense of accomplishment. One hurdle crossed at a time.

Chapter 9

Going Back to School

A fter a year at the Learning Center, I decided to try public school again. By now Michael was about eight years old and not wearing diapers. I thought the Learning Center was not providing enough academics or teaching him independence. However, I felt it did serve as a stepping stone in helping to prepare Michael to return to school. It provided a daily routine with other children. I wanted him to socialize with the other children, but he didn't play with them. He just watched them most of the time. The center did have a variety of children with various disabilities, but they were all low functioning, so no one interacted or played with each other. It seemed as if every child stayed in his or her own world.

Even when Michael attended the center, I continued to work with him every day, seven days a week. When I picked him up from the center, we went home and worked for 2 hours. I continued the hand and foot exercises from the therapists. By now Michael was getting tutored for sign language once a week for an hour.

By the end of the year, Michael was doing well. The aggression was down -- not totally gone, but better. He was urinating in the toilet by himself and asking me to take him to the bathroom. However, he was not having bowel movements in the toilet. I gave him an enema every day because I was afraid if I put the diaper back on, he would go back to urinating in the diaper and regress. I didn't want to have to train him all over again. I decided to tackle the pooping in the toilet another day. One problem at a time!

I decided to try public school again. By now Michael was in 2nd grade. I liked Michael's second grade teacher. She was very nice and allowed me to help her teach Michael and help her get to know what made him tick. I was there every step of the way, helping the teacher in any way I could. At this time, Michael's signs were modified because he was using only one hand. At school they were using picture symbols to help meet his needs.

That year, the school and the teacher kept a daily behavior chart on him to see the frequency of his aggression and what might cause it. I already knew that he became aggressive when he didn't want to do something, especially school work.

By the time Michael got to third grade, the aggression got so bad that he was hitting, scratching and biting the teachers and students. The school recommended a special center that helped children like Michael. When I visited the center, I saw a variety of students with different disabilities and classrooms. Every one had special needs. I said to myself, "Michael will revert back to his own world again". Michael needed to be around typical kids that would bring him into the real world.

Michael is non-verbal but, receptively, he understands what is happening around him and he likes to listen to and be around typical kids and adults. He knows the difference between handicapped kids and typical kids. He knows what he can and cannot do. He knows he is handicapped. He tells

69

me all the time that he is going to marry a normal girl, but his children will be handicapped. At the end of my visit to the center, I was standing by the exit door saying goodbye to the ESE (Exceptional Student Education) counselor, when suddenly a student, about 14 years old, walked up to me drooling and he slobbered saliva all over me and my sweater. The counselor waved his teacher over and handed him over to her. I smiled and said goodbye again. Even after I washed the sweater, it took me several days to stop smelling the odor. I realized this could be a good center; however, it was not a good fit for my Michael.

Chapter 10

Pooping in the Toilet, Not on the Floor

Getting Michael to urinate in the toilet was the easy part. By now Michael was eight years old. I was getting tired of giving him enemas every day. I had been giving Michael enemas since he was six years old. Before then he was wearing diapers, so he would sit on the floor and go in his diapers. When he was able to urinate in the toilet, I decided to take away the diapers all together. The problem was that every time he wanted to poop, he would sit on the floor.

Once he felt the urge to poop, he would sit anywhere. One time he was watching TV in his room and I came in to see how he was doing. Before I walked into the room, I smelled it. When I walked in, there was poop everywhere. He had smeared it on the TV, on his clothes, and it was coming out of the side of his shorts. So I decided to move the TV out of his room. I thought maybe he was enjoying the shows on the TV and he was too lazy to get up to use the bathroom. Now he had to watch TV in the family room where I could keep an eye on him.

When I left him in the family room, he still pooped on the floor. It got to a point where, if I saw him sitting on the floor I would get nervous and make him get up and sit on the chair. We didn't play any floor games or anything that required him to sit on the floor. Even when he went back to public school in 3rd grade, I told the teacher that by no means should she let Michael sit on the floor. If he sat on the floor, he might try to poop on the floor. I told her if the children sit on the floor during story time, please let Michael sit on a chair. There were some occasions in school where Michael slid down from his seat and pooped on the class floor. By the time the teacher noticed anything, the deed was done.

By now, I was giving him an enema every two days. I thought giving him an enema every day wasn't a good idea. But I noticed that the day that Michael did not get an enema he would become aggressive and have a bad day in school.

I decided to go back to giving him the enema every day. I didn't want the teachers to clean up that mess and deal with Michael's aggression.

I took Michael to a gastrologist to see if anything was wrong. I told the doctor that Michael would rather hold the poop in than to sit on the toilet. He prescribed a medication called MiraLAX. This medication was supposed to give Michael the urge to go so that he would not be able to hold the poop in. Michael, however, was able to hold in the poop for 3 to 4 days. Every day I would take him to the bathroom and he would just sit there and nothing would happen. If I left him alone, he would sit on the floor somewhere and poop on the floor.

I decided to take Michael out of school again after one year in third grade to try to teach him how to poop in the toilet, not the floor. I went back to my regular routine of teaching him math, reading, writing and potty training. By this time, I had hired a new behavior therapist that could help me with Michael. Since Michael was home now, we would have the time to do this. The first thing the therapist said to do was provide a time to make him sit on the toilet twice a day. With the medication giving him the urge and sitting on the toilet twice a day, I felt Michael was going to be able to do this. There I was wishfully thinking too fast.

A month went by and Michael was still not pooping in the toilet. We decided to change the strategy. The therapist told me to have Michael go on the floor, but in the bathroom. I told the therapist that when Michael was pooping on the floor, he got his body in this funny position with his left leg bent. Because he was semi-paralyzed on his right side, I think he needed that position to push.

She said we were going to create a toilet for him in the bathroom. From that toilet, we were going to transition him to a real toilet. First, she told me to make a circle on the bathroom floor using masking tape. The therapist said that the circle represented the lid on the toilet. I told Michael that he could poop on the floor, but only in the bathroom and he had to sit on the circle. I told Michael to remove his pants and keep his underwear on. This idea was actually working. I would see Michael sitting on the circle in the bathroom pooping with his underwear on. The drawback to this idea was the clean up. I did this for a week.

Next, I purchased an actual toilet lid and taped that to the floor. However, the lid was wobbly and did not stay on the floor. So we decided to use an 8x4 piece of drywall for him to sit on. Every week, I added another piece of wood. The goal was to keep adding the 8x4 drywall until it reached the height of the toilet. By 3 1/2 months, Michael was sitting on about 16 slaps of pieces of drywall. The problem with having so much drywall was cleaning each slap of wood. Michael would pee and poop in the underwear at the same time. The pee and the poop would be all over and in between the pieces of wood and sometimes he would smear it on the wall, his body and face. Do you know how hard it is to get poop out from under your fingernails? I would smell the poop for days.

Finally, we had my husband build a wide stool tall enough to push against the toilet, so when Michael sat on the actual toilet his body would be on same level. We wanted to simulate the feel of sitting on floor. Like everything else in life, you can't win them all.

After 5 months of this ordeal, Michael did not poop in the toilet. He still got an enema every day. I decided to stop.

I was thinking that maybe he was not ready. I decided to leave the bowel movement process alone and tackle it another time.

Chapter 11

Building Brain Power

My friend had told me about a program called the National Association for Child Development (NACD) that she was using with her daughter and she felt was working. She said her daughter was more focused when doing an activity and her memory had improved with the program. At this point, I was willing to try almost anything. I thought I would build on what Michael knew and increase his intelligence, which would help with his maturity and, in turn, help him with self-control.

Under this program, I introduced 15 to 20 words a week, working with words and signing them four times a day. First thing in the morning, before breakfast, in the car, before lunch, any time. We would play memory games. I would say three to four items and he would have to say them back to me in the order or sequence that I said. Everything was a teachable moment. A simple conversation would grow into a major topic by asking, "Why?" "Why do you say that?" "What else would you do?"

Before that, Michael's conversations were simple. He would sign one to two words only and his response was one word. We talked about everything, from religion to politics. I don't know how much he understood, but I tried to explain in words to help him understand. If he didn't understand something, he would ask, "Why?"

By the time we started this program, I had been home schooling Michael for two years. I saw tremendous improvement within that time. With this improvement, I thought he was ready to go back to school. By now Michael was 11 years old. When I took him back to elementary school, I was told he needed to go to middle school. There was no way that Michael was ready for middle school. So I told the school that I wanted to keep him back one year. I wanted him to have the last year in elementary school so the transition to middle school would be easier. That would give me the time to prepare him. I was also working with a child psychologist to help with his behavior.

That last year in elementary school, we talked about going to a "big boy school, not a baby school." I would drive by the middle school every day and say how wonderful the school was and how his big sister Brittany went there and she loved it. His cousins Jason, Tina and Steven all went there and they had fun. We would ride our bikes there and show him the entrance of the school.

Michael had a good first year in middle school.

Chapter 12

Providing Normalcy for My Daughter, Brittany

From day one, I wanted to set the atmosphere and tone for Brittany to see Michael as her little brother. Not her handicapped brother, not a retarded brother or a problem brother, only her little brother that she was going to love and protect, no matter what. Brittany was five years old when I was pregnant. One day, I asked her what name would she give her baby brother, and she said Michael. I asked, "Why Michael?" She said, "My best friend's brother is named Michael."

As soon as I realized that there was something wrong with Michael, I made up my mind that I wasn't going to treat him any differently than my daughter. So what if he walked funny, and grunted when he tried to speak, I was determined that my daughter, nieces, nephews and other children in the family were not going to be scared of him. I was able to teach Brittany and my niece Tina some sign language because they were around Michael more and played with him more. When the children were playing, I had Michael sit next to them. Even if he couldn't participate, he would watch them and see how typical kids interacted.

As a little girl, Brittany was very sociable and friendly. She had birthday parties every year and had sleepovers with her friends. All her friends were very sweet and kind to Michael. As she got older, however, and started bringing new friends to the house, I noticed a surprised look on her friends' faces when they first met Michael. After her friends left, I would ask her why she didn't tell them and if they even knew she had a brother. I was shocked at her answer. She said, "My friends know I have a brother, but I don't tell them that he's handicapped." She said, "To me, Michael is not handicapped. He can communicate, he can play and he understands everything I say. He is able to do much more than some other children that are handicapped. He just can't talk with his mouth. So to me, he is normal."

I had always told her, "You and your brother are a package deal. The man you choose to marry must also love your brother. If he doesn't like your brother, he is not worth your time or energy. He will not be able to love and care for you."

At home, Brittany and Michael interact like any brother and sister. Michael loves getting Brittany into trouble. He would tell me by signing that Brittany didn't make her bed this morning, or didn't do the dishes. If you asked him what Brittany liked to do, he would say that she loved talking on the phone. Brittany would scream at him and say, "Stop telling on me. You talk too much!"

Sometimes I would laugh to myself and say "Wow." She really sees him as her little brother.

Chapter 13

My Daily Struggles

The second year in middle school was difficult. He was having a rough time. I don't know if it was the hormones or just being a teenager. That school year, Michael became more aggressive at school and at home. At school, he was hitting the students, grabbing them and pulling the girls' hair.

One day, when I picked him up from school, the teacher told me that he refused to do his work and she gave me the work so he could finish it at home. By then, Michael knew when I was not happy with him. We walked out of the school and into the van. On our way home, I didn't talk to him. I didn't give him any attention. When I pulled into the driveway, he signed to me that he wanted to watch TV. I told him that he had to finish all of his work first. Well, he gave me that look, the look that says, "I'm not doing it and you can't make me." He turned his head to the side looked down and shut me out. That's when the battle of the wills began.

I opened his door for him to get out and I walked inside the house. The behaviorist told me to ignore him when he acted like that. I told him what he had to do before he could watch TV. That day, Michael stayed in the car for three hours with the door open, the same way I had left him. When he finally came into the house, he walked up to me and signed, "Can I watch TV?"

Out loud, I said, "You've got to be kidding me! Your work comes first." Then he tried to hit me, so I took him by the arm and walked very quickly to his room. I knew that, if I didn't do that, he would drop his body to the floor and I wouldn't be able to move him.

With all of the aggravation and his stubbornness, I try not to get angry. But sometimes it's hard not to. When I feel like I'm getting depressed or feeling sorry for myself, I think about the children who are worse off than Michael and that mother's pain. Then I realize I have no right to be depressed or sad. If I dwell on this temporary situation, then I am devaluing someone with a more serious, more dire situation. This makes me snap out of my self-pity very quickly.

Chapter 14

What's Michael Doing Now?

I heard a great sermon one day. In the sermon, the preacher was talking about fear. He said, "In order to have courage, you need fear." The statement got my attention and I wanted to hear more. He continued with, "You need courage to do the very thing that you are scared of doing. If you were not afraid, it would be easy. You would not need courage to do something that is easy." Whoa!

Michael is fifteen now and will start high school this year and I am very, very afraid. I took him to meet his teacher a couple of days before school started. I told her all about Michael's aggression and things that he is able to do and how I work with him at home. I also gave her suggestions and strategies to protect herself from his aggression and attacks.

I told her to look out for certain facial expressions that can warn of his behavior ahead of time.

For example, if you're talking to him and suddenly he doesn't respond and puts his head down and his hands together, that's a bad sign. You should not approach him when he looks like that. However, if you do, put your hand on his right arm (this is his only working arm) and talk calmly and softly. Then he knows that you are not mad at him. His attention span is between 20 – 30 minutes long with activities that he likes.

I told her about the last two years in middle school. As a matter of fact, I told her I had to take him out of school a month before school ended due to his aggression. I took him off of zoloft and respidone, the aggression medication that he had been on for the past two and a half years because they were not helping.

I am happy to say that Michael is now able to urinate on his own and have a bowel movement on his own most of the time. I do give him an enema occasionally. Using his favorite things like the I-Touch, music and TV as motivators, his behavior has gotten much better. He can read on a second grade level and he loves watching female wrestling.

A couple of days ago, my husband and I heard a sound around three o'clock in the morning. My husband said to me, "Is that Michael peeing in the bathroom?" We heard him flush and walk back to his room and close the door. My husband said, "I thought I would never see this day."

I said, "I know. Isn't it wonderful?"

Michael has helped me become a better person. He has made me search within and confront myself. I am now more conscious of the feelings of others, more understanding, and I have a new level of awareness of what's important in life. He is my constant reminder to always be gracious and grateful. I now realize what a miracle it is when I see children talking, walking, and running. I love and appreciate life. These new insights have changed my life. I now speak with a level of understanding that I didn't have before. When I look back at my life, I see that I was preparing to become a teacher without even realizing it. I didn't know God was going to give me Michael to help in my transformation. Michael is my wonderful reminder of the great and beautiful things in life. I am blessed to have uncovered my hidden gift

-- my son, Michael.

Chapter 15

My Praying Grandmother

My grandmother is 100 years old. She grew up poor in the countryside of Haiti. She had to stop going to school in the second grade in order to help her family. My grandmother doesn't know how to read or write. She traveled to the city with her mother or father to sell straw hats to tourists and the locals.

She told me that she was saved and accepted Jesus Christ into her life when she was about 12 years old. She has never worn pants, make-up, or jewelry. She is a very religious woman. She is constantly praying for the family and strangers. I take her shopping once a month to buy her groceries. Every time she gets into my car and we're driving to the store or anywhere, she looks at the cars driving by and starts praying. She prays the same prayer all the time. She says,

"God, I pray that you bring these people home safely to their families."

I asked her once, "Why do you do that?" She said that they needed it. I said to myself, *These people don't even know that they have a grandmother praying for them.* I wonder what they would say or what they would think if they knew.

She told me that one day my son Michael will talk and she will see it before she dies. I looked at her in a crazy way and said, "Grandma, you are 100 years old. This had better happen quickly, because there's not much time left." She laughed at me when I said that. She said that I'm not praying hard enough or I don't have enough faith. I told her, "It doesn't matter whether I have enough faith or not; it is up to God to make Michael talk. It is up to God's will if he wants Michael to talk. He may want Michael to stay the way he is. Am I going to tell God he's wrong? He knows what's best for me."

What I do pray for is for God to give me strength to handle what He has given me. He knows what I want and what is in my heart. Why should I constantly bother Him with something He already knows? There are people that need Him more than I do. I would hope He would give comfort to the mother with the baby that is dying of cancer, and the family that is starving and hasn't eaten in a week. These people need Him more than I do. My son can walk, he understands when I talk to him, and he's healthy. Why would I bother God with my selfishness? I should only say, "Thank you," a million times over and show my gratitude.

I'm not sure my grandmother understands my thinking. However, she continues to tell me about increasing my faith and to pray for a miracle. And I continue to tell her that I already have one.

Part 2:

Personal Stories from Family and Friends

Chapter 16

Thanks, Steve Jobs!

By Jean Augustin

I never truly appreciated the personal impact of technology until we gave our son, Michael, his first I-Touch. I could not imagine how this simple device would change his life, open his world and give him a voice. The common view is that these devices, coupled with the growth of access to the Internet, have democratized the world, changed lives, toppled governments and empowered many who did not have a voice before. I never really believed that statement, preferring to see most technology as a vehicle of an increasingly narcissistic society. Personally, I resisted most technological trends until I had no other choice. I never played computer games growing up, even PAC-Man. I begrudgingly got an email account and Internet access only when I started to commute to New York from Fort Lauderdale in 2001. I refused to carry a Blackberry after 6pm because I believed it intruded on my personal life and turned me into a 24-hour employee without any additional remuneration from my employer. Although I now accept the new cyber reality, I continue to hold out against social media. Having said all of that, I will admit that technology -- Apple in particular -- has completely changed my son's life in the most profound way.

Michael's behavior always puzzled me. I cried, prayed, begged and bargained with God to give him a voice, or at least pacify him. He can be charming, manipulative, angry, impatient, sad, frustrated, loving, scared and sensitive all at the same time. He has a unique personality and innate intelligence, tragically trapped inside a body that refuses to cooperate. To deal with his aggression, his physicians recommended several mood-altering drugs with severe side effects. We hated numbing him, but at times we had no other choice. His mom learned through sign language that he created an alternate reality in his mind that mirrored our real world.

In this imaginary world, he also traveled to New York weekly for work. He had a beautiful girlfriend who strangely looked and acted like his mom, and he had several imaginary children. By the way, his children were also disabled. Michael understands that he is different and cannot speak. He needed to keep in contact with the children by text, so we broke off the cover of an old English to Spanish translator, gave it to him and he used it as a texting device.

Shortly after, as he felt the difference between real phones -- especially the Blackberry -- and the translator, he only wanted a real phone. Whenever he found a cell phone lying around, he would use it to text his "guy friend" and girl friend. Soon, we could not leave a phone anywhere. He would inadvertently dial names on the phone by mistake or even delete contacts. We started asking family and friends to donate old Blackberry devices for him to use. He likes Blackberries the most because the keys are elevated and he can type with one hand.

Over time, the make believe texting morphed into his single greatest passion. When we finally gave him his first

Itouch, it was his liberation. His life had changed and he was finally empowered. I guess the media was right after all.

We started out by asking all family members and friends for used I-Touches and iPhones. My sister donated her old iPhone 3. My daughter gave us her first generation Itouch, since she got a free I-Touch when she purchased the I-MAC. Her boyfriend forgot his Itouch at the house and, when she got into a lover's quarrel with him, she gave it to Mike. Good luck getting it back, buddy.

We started accumulating used Itouches. Soon, we had an equally large "Itouch cemetery." Some had broken screens and others simply could not power on. I don't believe the developers at Apple ever imagined the amount of abuse that Mike could inflict on the Itouch. We should send them a You-Tube video. I am sure that their product testing team would invite him to California to perform stress test and product control. He can literally spend 8 hours pressing the same key.

Finally, we had no other choice than to start buying Itouches. We purchased the first Itouch from Sam's Club to save a few dollars. We also purchased a case and screen protector. The case did not survive the drive home. We then realized that he loved the feeling of the bare Itouch. Remember that he only has one good hand. We tried to prepare ourselves for the inevitable accidents. Unfortunately, without a protective case, the Itouch screen was no match for our tile floors. We had an equally tough time with headsets.

Mike can't resist cords. He twirls them around his fingers and finally, when frustrated, he holds the head piece in his mouth and destroys the headset. I bought him a pair of Skull Candy headsets. They looked so cool and were appropriate for a teenager. They lasted 2 days. Mike can't resist strings, cords or laces. It's not fair to tempt him like this.

Soon, while working in New York, I started receiving frantic calls from Suzy. He got bored and tore the cord on the headset. He bumped into someone at school and broke the screen on the Itouch. Consequently, he would not have the Itouch or headset until we could buy replacements. All hell would break loose until the world was made right again. I decided that I needed to resolve this situation.

Suzy can handle anything with Mike and tried not to increase my burden while working in New York. But even

Wonder Woman could not control Mike when he was "Jonesing" for this potent and addiction drug.

Eureka moment! I saw a jogger near the Apple flagship store on Fifth Avenue with a wireless headset. I decided that it must be Bluetooth. I ventured into the glass box entrance, which reminds me of the entrance to the Louvre in Paris, determined to have a wireless Bluetooth headset and to confirm that it would work with the Itouch. Confirmed! There is a God.

As soon as I got home that weekend, we rushed to Best Buy to purchase a new Itouch and Bluetooth headset. I spoke with one of the young tech support guys and explained our problem. Cases would not work. The young tech insisted that Mike could not destroy the Military Spec case. For heaven's sake, it survived tours in Iraq. By the way, the young man then made an error that should get him fired by BestBuy. He offered us replacement insurance on the Itouch, regardless of the kind of damage: water, mechanical, software or Mike. For a mere $37 we could bring the damaged Itouch and get a brand new replacement. No questions asked. Then we could buy replacement insurance on the new one for $37.

At this point, we were purchasing a new Itouch per month at a price of $200. I believe we were up to seven units ($1,400). Although that is crazy by most standards, I still thought it was a bargain. The joy and calming effect that the Itouch gave Mike was priceless. We were paying $280 per month for music therapy, but the therapist moved to LA to pursue a music career. *Heck,* I figured, *even without insurance, I would now save $80 per month.* With the replacement plan, I would now save $175 per month. This was a no-brainer.

I paid for the insurance on the Itouch. Then the tech support guy told me that we could get insurance on the Bluetooth headset as well. But this deal was even better. The headset cost $59 and the insurance was $11 for 2 years. I just had to bring the broken headset to the return area and get a new one. Let's see, that is $59 times 24 months for a whopping $1,416 in headsets for $11. God bless BestBuy; I hope they stay in business.

"We should get you a BestBuy ID." That is a recent statement made by a security guard at the entrance of BestBuy. Imagine the embarrassment of returning an Itouch or Bluetooth headset every month to the same store. At the counter, the clerk does not ask the reason you are returning the item. Suzy has always been stronger than I am when it comes to Mike. Although she had some initial embarrassment, she quickly got over it. On the other hand, I try to never return the Itouch, or I at least hope it breaks during the week when I am in New York traveling. I feel the need to pull the "disabled card" whenever I return either item. I start the conversation by telling the clerk that my disabled son broke it. As Suzy would say "Do you think she cares? Just suck it up and return it."

The Itouch is now a vital part of our lives. It is Mike's window to the world. Even though his reading skills are minimal, he can search through 1,600 songs to find the Lenny Kravitz' song *Are You Going My Way*. He uses the Itouch to motivate him and put him in the "zone" while riding is tricycle. The Itouch has also given me a common device that binds us closer together. We use the FaceTime app while I'm in New York to video chat with Mike. He can simply launch the FaceTime app all by himself and video call with me or his sister Brittany. Unbelievable! There are so many ways for Mike to use the Itouch, from games to speech apps. I only have one complaint. Mike loves the Itouch so much that he wakes up at 2:30 am to use it. Please create an I Sleep app! Thank you, Steve Jobs!

Chapter 17

Sunday Lunches with Michael

By Uncle Ronald

Sunday lunches with Michael started as a reward for his being good in school. As it turns out, it's been my reward to spend time with such an innocent little boy who has changed all of our lives. Simply put, Michael has made me realize the important things in life. Most people worry about losing their jobs or not getting a specific task completed. They agonize about it and worry to point of hysteria. I understand this is important to most people and I am not minimizing their feelings. I am only suggesting adopting a different perspective on life. I believe this outlook will bring more meaning to their lives, both professionally and personally. I have shared my experiences and relationship with Michael with many of my colleagues and friends. I hope they will understand me better and I hope I have changed their perspective in a small way.

Being part of Michael's routine has made me feel good about myself. This is the selfish part of helping someone, and I don't think there's anything wrong with that.

I have heard many people say children like Michael are gifts to the world. I am still trying to understand this. Is it really a gift, or do we feel good by saying it? I believe many people say it as a means of coping with their situation. How else can you justify it? I hear people say "Why me?" Well, why not you? However, I do believe the parents and caretakers of these special children deserve a special place in our hearts. These children deserve our love, support and admiration for their courage.

I always look forward to our Sunday lunches. I am always anxious that Michael was not good during the week and, therefore, no lunch. Our adventure starts with a call to his mother. Once I have the "OK," I pick him up at his house. You should see the excitement in his face when I show up.

He gives me a hug and a kiss and, of course, he wants to arm wrestle me. I grab his cup and off we go to the pizza parlor.

In the car, Michael has the radio blasting and he wants the sunroof open. I always oblige; it's his day. By the way, that's all we ever eat – PIZZA. We get to the neighborhood restaurant and everyone knows us. Everyone greets Michael. We sit in the same booth, with Michael facing the television on the wall. By the time we sit down, the chef is already making the slice of Sicilian pizza for Michael and the waiter/ waitress brings me a Corona beer. Mike takes his cup and we do a toast. Michael always tells me that drinking is not good and gives him a headache. I wonder where he got that from (DAD??).

After lunch, we go for ice cream at McDonald's. The workers at the restaurant always assume Michael is my son. I really enjoy my time together with Michael and I will do my best to continue this tradition. I don't know what Michael gets out of these lunches, but I hope he sees me as a constant in his life, like his parents.

It is very easy to be Michael's uncle. I get to spend time with him, but I can go home afterward and leave the hard work for his mom, dad and sister. Michael is their world, their reality. How do they cope and live with this? They cannot do this alone. Uncle Ronald to the rescue? No. I am not special for having a lunch date with my nephew. His parents and sister are special.

I have a great deal of respect and admiration for Michael's mom. This is a cliché, but she is the glue that holds this family together. Mothers are truly special. Fathers are special too, but just not that special. Imagine the frustration of a little boy that cannot speak and communicate his feelings and thoughts with you. I have witnessed the pain in my brother's face sometimes when he speaks about Michael's bad day in school. Nothing I can say or do can ease that pain or the reality of the situation. I can only offer my support and let him and my sister in-law know I am here for them. I will never say I understand; I don't live in their reality.

I was watching ESPN one day and they did a special on a young man that was blind and learned how to shoot free throws from his older brother. This young man was born blind and his eyes were eventually removed, but not his spirit. His older brother was the coach of a team and for one game -- a championship game -- he was allowed to shoot all of the free throws for the team. The entire team decided on this. The game was very close. He had missed six previous shots and, with the game on the line at the end, he made two free throws to win it. This is an example of what people like this young man and Michael go through, and yet they are positive and succeed. There are a lot of special people in the world. These are the heroes of the world, people like this young man and Michael.

I have absolutely no patience for healthy, able bodied people that ruin their lives by their own doing. Most people take things for granted. Michael will never run, he will never speak, never tie his shoelaces, will never drive a car. Just think about this for a second; these are things most of us have done or will do. However, we take these things for granted.

I promise one thing to Michael and his parents – I will always be there for them. As for now, I'm looking forward to my next Sunday lunch with my buddy, Michael.

Chapter 18

The Michael Effect

By Auntie Maggie

My name is Maggie Augustin and I am the proud aunt of Michael Augustin. I remember the day Suzy called me and asked if I could come and check Mike's eyes. She said his eye looked "strange." I rushed over to her house and realized one pupil was not reacting to light. Suzy was concerned and I did not want to alarm her or make her any more upset than she was. It was a Sunday afternoon and, as calmly as possible, I asked her to call her pediatrician in the morning and request a visit. Suzy called her pediatrician and Mike was seen immediately.

The pediatrician ordered multiple diagnostic exams and the whole family waited anxiously for the results. I remember rushing home from work to wait in my in-laws home for the results. As a nurse, my initial thoughts were of a catastrophic nature; brain tumor, cancer and a possible stroke. The MRI (Magnetic Resonance Imaging, a test that uses a magnetic field and pulses of radio wave energy to take pictures of the head)ruled out my worst fears, but was unable to offer a definitive answer to Mike's symptoms. Later, Mike was diagnosed with cerebral palsy, brain injury and tortocollis. After Mike's diagnosis, Suzy and Jean's lives would never be the same.

Michael is loving, sensitive and a very affectionate young man. It is very difficult to be in Mike's presence and not smile and feel his genuine love for people. When Mike was an infant, his needs were the same as any infant. As Mike grew, so did his many challenges. Mike was not meeting any of the age-appropriate milestones, such as babbling, crawling and potty training.

As a toddler, Mike was not able to walk; he required a special walker and stroller. Mike was unable to drink out of a cup and required a special drinking cup. Suzy later asked me to help with potty-training. Mike required an enema to assist with bowel movements. Mike and Suzy made a special name in sign language for me which translated to "Auntie Butt." We still get a good laugh at that. That was the beginning of my special relationship with Mike.

When you are in Mike's presence, it is all about Mike. He requires your undivided attention. Mike likes to arm wrestle. He will arm wrestle anyone at anytime to see who is stronger, and he is willing to cheat to win. Mike is non-verbal, and most of us have limited ability to use sign language to communicate with him. That does not stop Mike's attempt to communicate with us. He enjoys signing how silly someone is because he realizes that we all know that phrase.

I often wonder if Mike knows how special he is. He was able to communicate to Suzy that his arm and legs do not work well. He shared with Suzy that when he gets married and has children, their arms and legs won't work either. His perception of his handicap would often break my heart; and then I realized that Mike is not sad about his deficits. He accepts his handicap; his inability to complete most tasks does not affect his self image. If you ask Mike if he is strong, smart, or handsome, the answer is always an emphatic "Yes."

As parents, we all wish and pray for healthy children. I often imagine what it is like to be the parent of a special needs child. What happens when some parents are given children with special needs? Did God not hear their prayers? I will never know the pain, worry and disappointment associated with having a special needs child. I often wonder, "Do the parents of a special needs child mourn the loss of all the possible accomplishments, future grandchildren, and potential contribution to society, in order to celebrate the small but monumental achievements?"

Following Mike's diagnosis, I witnessed the initial shock, followed by anger, then despair and finally acceptance from Suzy. Suzy set the tone for Mike's quality of life. She was determined that Mike would have a voice. She had a vision for Mike's future and she encouraged all of the family members to support her vision.

Mike's relationship with his cousins has made them more compassionate and caring. I take great joy in any of Mike's minor accomplishments. I fully appreciate how challenging it is for Mike to walk, have bowel movements and perform daily activities. Handicapped people do not need our pity. They deserve our respect and attention. The next time you see a handicapped person, smile and say "Hello." Don't stare; give them some support.

Because of Mike, I am a stronger advocate for the disabled and those in need. I am more sensitive to the needs of children without a voice. Mike reminds me to be happy, because he is.

Chapter 19

My Role as Auntie

By Auntie Mariane

I am Michael's aunt, Mariane. I moved to South Florida to live with my parents and attend nursing school shortly before Michael was born in 1995. The extended family -- which includes my parents and I, my brothers and their respective wives and children -- all lived within a one mile radius of each other. When Michael was born everything seemed normal, but as he grew and months went by, the family as a whole became aware of his developmental issues.

Our family has always been close, so it was particularly difficult for my parents and I to watch the pain and difficulties that both my brother and sister-in-law were encountering while raising a special needs child. It was just as painful to see this beautiful child struggle through each developmental stage, but it was absolutely delightful when he reached and conquered the smallest milestones. We would all watch in awe when he did the simplest of things, because for us it meant he was getting closer to "normal." Since discovering Michael's special needs, each member of this family has played a role in his life.

My role in Michael's life has been primarily as a concerned aunt, but has also been as a health care professional. I received my Bachelor's degree in Nursing when Michael was two years old, but shortly after that returned to school to become an occupational therapist. Becoming an occupational therapist was a goal I had had since early college after completing volunteer work in a nursing home/rehab center where my father worked. I received a Masters in Occupational Therapy during Michael's early childhood years.

Occupational, physical and speech services are integral parts of treatment for a developmentally disabled child, so you might think that I became some sort of wonder therapist for Michael. The truth is that most of my experience (in nursing and in occupational therapy) has always been with adults, specifically geriatrics. My experience with pediatrics has always been very general and limited.

Quite frankly, as much as I love kids, I always found it difficult to work with the pediatric population. It takes an unusual amount of patience, skill, strength and creativity. It can also be very tedious, specifically because the goals set for the child are often small to start with and may remain that way for some time, meaning the progress seen can be very small, but extremely significant.

Working with a special needs child requires great patience because the special needs child does not respond in the same manner as a typical child. The child's behavior can often lie outside the norms of a typical child's behavior. Behavioral reactions can be extreme and aggressive, even to the simplest change in routine or environmental stimuli.

Skill is required to handle the child appropriately and to implement techniques that facilitate improved functioning. Skill is integral on the part of the therapist, specifically in providing caregiver education to confused and often frightened parents who need to learn how to effectively interact with and assist their child. As a therapist, emotional strength is imperative to keep from becoming swept up in the sadness that will often arise when dealing with a suffering child and emotionally fragile parents.

Finally, occupational therapists who work with pediatric clients must have a creative approach. Occupational therapy for children encompasses an array of areas; however the base of its approach involves play. Engaging the child in play to determine where there are limitations and to ascertain current function is a common approach to assessment or evaluation and to treating the child.

Although I had limited experience with pediatrics, I did become involved in providing assistance to my sister-in-law, who acted as primary caregiver to Michael. Sometimes that involved providing professional recommendations or insight. Sometimes it involved ordering specialized devices or equipment to adapt and facilitate increased independence for Michael. I remember specifically fabricating a special splint which would protect his skin from further injury due to frequent hand chewing (a behavior Michael often engaged in as a self-stimulating/self soothing mechanism).

117

Finally, I would say my role in Michael's life has also been as a source for my own parents. My parents have been wonderful grandparents to all of their grandchildren; however, with Michael it would be undeniably different and challenging. Because they have been very involved in Michael's care, part of my role has been in helping them understand Michael's condition in terms of his strengths, his limitations, his behaviors and the best ways to interact with him.

Over the years I have watched Michael grow from a baby into a toddler, into early childhood and now into a teenager. As a therapist, I can say that I have witnessed tremendous gains (thanks to the diligence and dedication of my sister-in-law, Suzy) and the early intervention he has received. I've seen Michael's communication skills (through sign language) explode and his participation in his own self-care increase exponentially. I've seen his sense of humor and reasoning develop, and most importantly I've watched him form amazing bonds with each member of the family. Although it has been pleasure to watch Michael grow and become the kid he is today, he continues to have tremendous needs which are challenging on an almost daily basis. This is a fact of life in our family. Michael may never be what is defined as "normal," but what he is to me as an aunt and to the rest of the family is "extraordinary."

Chapter 20

A Silent Influence

By Christina Augustin

My name is Tina and I'm Michael's cousin. All my life, I never consciously thought about Michael's effect on my life. Until reflecting upon it today, I think I would have said my life wouldn't have been any different if he was born normal.

Being only three years older than he is, I can't remember what life was like before he was born. There's always been a sense of normalcy in his condition and I honestly think that throughout my childhood -- perhaps even to the age of 8 or 9 -- I never really knew there was something wrong. Maybe this was why I was always commended for playing with him as a child, and why the sign for my name translated means "near his heart." I think I always tried to treat him like a normal kid, rather than like baby him or treat him differently, as some people do, even if not purposely. All of this being said, I realize now that I would be wrong to say that Michael didn't have any effect on my life, even if at first it went unnoticed.

I remember it vividly, as if it were yesterday. It was such a memorable time. One day my Auntie Suzy and I went to pick up Michael from school. This school was a special center for non-verbal children. In this school they had a two-way mirror where parents could watch the children during their lessons or at play. At first we watched and observed the children (all handicapped) playing in their classroom.

Looking at their faces, into their eyes, you could see the happiness emanating. The simplest games and toys brought them joy, as if their disabilities didn't matter. To them, it seemed as if those simple moments of bliss were enough. That day I left the school with a completely new outlook on life. These children taught me a lesson about gratitude. How could I, or anyone with no restrictions, dare to be unhappy when these children, constrained by all kinds of disabilities

-- physical and mental -- could maintain their happiness? That, right there, was an influence Michael had on me without my notice.

After much reflection, I realize now that I wouldn't be the person that I am today if Michael weren't the way *he* is. I am more patient, more tolerant, more respectful, and more gracious. Although I never really comprehended his effect on my life, I see now that he has always been a silent influence on my character.

Chapter 21

My perspective

By Brittany Augustin

My brother puts my life into perspective. In a way, he is like that little angel on my shoulder that is always reminding me of what I should do, who I should be, and what I should be thankful for. When I was younger, Michael's disabilities really didn't have much of an effect on me. For some reason, as a child I really didn't notice his differences and I can honestly say that I had a normal and fun-filled childhood and I never felt that my family was different from others. As I got older, I realized he had disabilities but I still was never embarrassed of him. My brother and my family have always been the most important thing in everything I do, such as my behavior and hard work, and even my grades in school. I do the best I can so that I will make my parents and Michael proud.

My brother won't be able to do the things that I will be able to do so, for him, I will never throw away any opportunities. If I act stupidly and ruin my life, it would be like slapping Michael in the face and I would never do that. Knowing this, when I went away to college I chose to focus instead of falling into college ways and going crazy with drugs and alcohol. I want to be successful to be able to give my brother and myself a good life in the future.

I've been kind of a second mother to Michael; at least that's what my family members say to me. I was always my mother's right hand during his potty training and "hitting" days. I've learned responsibility, appreciation, kindness, and patience from my brother and I like that I was able to grow up learning so much. Being Michael's older sister, I think is why I am and still strive to be a good person.

At this point of my life, I'm still growing up. So as I look into the future, I am nervous that one day I will take full responsibility for Michael. Taking care of him means devoting your life to him just like my mom does, but since I'm only

20 years old right now, I am in a pretty selfish state of mind. I want to travel and I want to live separately from my parents. Nevertheless, I have no fear that when I'm ready, I will take care of Michael. I think that I am more special because I have a special brother. I feel that I have a larger grasp on what life means than my peers and I am thankful for that outlook on life.

Chapter 22

My Summer Vacation with Michael

By Tatiana Franklin

My name is Tatiana and I'm Michael's 15 year-old cousin. For the past three years, I've been spending my summer vacations with my auntie Suzy, Uncle Jean, and cousins Brittany and Michael in Florida. Sometimes I help Auntie Suzy tutor Michael. During the summer we go to movies, we play in the pool and sometimes we get up early and Auntie Suzy picks up my other cousins and takes all of us to breakfast.

I remember when I was very little and Michael snatched my pretzel and took a bite of it (or at least, he tried to). His older sister Brittany snatched it back and I found it a bit deformed and covered with some saliva. All I thought was, "Ew!" See, no one had ever really told me what was "wrong" with Michael, so I just thought he was...extremely weird. That is, until I got a little older.

I started to realize and understand on my own that Michael was different. Then the adults in my family tried to explain it to me and teach me how to interact with him correctly. And now, well, I realize that Michael isn't different at all. He loves listening to music, just like me. He likes goof-dancing, just like me. He likes to laugh a lot, just like me. He watches shows that his mother believes are inappropriate, just like me. His mother hates the *Jerry Springer Show*, as do I and everyone else, but I absolutely love seeing Michael laugh hysterically and have the happiest eyes while watching it. He loves this show. I think he likes to see the people fight. When he turns on the show, I can hear my Auntie Suzy scream from her room yelling, "SHUT THAT THING OFF!" and instead of turning the TV off, he just lowers the volume.

Michael is a regular teenager who just needs a little more attention and care-taking than most. But overall, he's one of the funniest and greatest kids I will ever come to meet. He's also the best arm-wrestler I will ever meet. Interacting with Michael isn't very different than with any other little kid, or even teen, that I know. Anything I say or do will make him smile, which makes my day every day that I am with him. We can carry a full conversation about anything or nothing at all, just as if he were one of my best friends.

Yes, it does require taking things slowly with him, physically. But it allows me to gain patience with him and everybody else. It's a good thing too, because tutoring him can sometimes be a hassle. Michael is a mega jokester and he'll always act like he's falling asleep when we're doing a lesson. But as soon as I or his mom mentions a sandwich or ice cream, he pops awake right away. He may be a double handful to deal with at times, but it's definitely worth it to have someone like Michael in my life.

Chapter 23

Interacting with Michael

By Barbara Dubois

My friend Suzy asked me to write a few words about her son Michael, who was born with disabilities. I thought about this for a long time, as I was not sure what to write or how to express how I have felt about knowing Michael.

I guess I will start at the beginning. When I first found out that Suzy and Jean's son had these disabilities and would be like this for the rest of his life, I really thought of my friends first. I was terribly worried and full of sorrow for them. I thought a family of such a child knows shock, grief, sadness, fear, worry and uncertainty. But I have learned throughout the years that they also know great love; more love, I believe, than most families. I have seen with Jean and Suzy that they know that each milestone, each step taken toward the future is a positive one. And each step back, although (I imagine) a heart-ache at times, is a challenge to be conquered. And conquer my friend Suzy has. I applaud her. I admire her strength and tenacity.

Now, when I first began to interact with Michael, I really thought of his feelings. I wondered how much he understood and how he must feel. I wanted him to be comfortable around me and I did not want him to feel different. So I set about doing what I thought was best for our relationship, and that was trying to be myself as much as I could with Mike. It turns out that it was not that difficult. Mike seemed to like me from the start. He would hold my hand and kiss it. He is always smiling and has a sense of humor, I discovered. Don't get me wrong -- there were times when he threw some serious temper tantrums. But, honestly, what child doesn't when he does not get his way?

I remember one occasion when we all went on vacation together. We went on a cruise and Mike was with us. He had these beads that he played with; he always had them in his hand. According to Suzy and Jean, this kept him calm and if they lost the beads...well, we would be in trouble. Of course, we lost the beads! I don't remember how we lost them, but all of a sudden they were gone and Suzy and Jean were panicking. All I kept hearing was that we had to find the beads or purchase others. I remember thinking to myself, *How bad could this really be? We will just have to find him something else to play with.* Well, I was wrong.

I soon found out that this was serious and we really had to find the beads. Everyone who was not keeping Mike busy had one task and only one task and that was to find the beads or find beads to purchase! I really felt bad because I kept thinking, *What will happen if we do not find these beads? We are in the middle of the ocean, after all, on a ship full of people.* This was one of the times I realized how hard it was caring for a child with a disability. We did not want Mike to become upset, as it would be difficult to calm him down again. His uncle did find a small shop on the ship and was able to purchase some beads there. Mike never even knew that his beads had gone missing.

Mike is a great kid. I learned that it doesn't matter if his progress may be slow, his accomplishments may not show as quickly as those of other kids and he does require extra care -- he is a lovely child. God put him here. Loving a disabled person is a blessing; I really do believe that. It is not difficult.

I know what it's like to have someone in your family who is different. You see, my mom was blind, but she was the greatest inspiration in my life. There is always something appealing and interesting about every person if you look hard enough, and Mike is no different. I guess I have always tried to see what about Mike is the same as other children rather than what is different. I hope that he has felt that throughout my interactions with him. I hope he has felt understood, for the most part. I hope he has felt respected and -- more than anything -- accepted as he is, and loved.

Chapter 24

Lessons Learned

By Sariah Dodier

My name is Sariah. I am Michael's nineteen-year–old cousin. A lot of people don't know much about disabled kids, or about people in general. In 1999, I had my first real encounter with someone who is disabled, but it happened to be family -- my own cousin, Michael.

I was only 7 years old when I first met Michael and, honestly, I was freaked out by him. I don't know why; maybe because I had never met anyone like him before, or didn't know how to talk to him or anything. But that changed quickly. Moving to Florida from Brooklyn was a new experience for me, but meeting Michael was a whole new chapter and gave me a new outlook on life.

I grew close to my cousins Brittany and Christina -- they were like my best friends growing up -- and Michael was Brittany's little brother. Brittany is the oldest girl out of us three, so I always looked up to her. She was two years older, and Christina and I were just a couple months apart. I spent almost every weekend with them and began to watch how Auntie Suzy and my cousins talked to Michael. They used sign language and, little by little, they taught me signs so I could start interacting with Michael.

I remember one weekend my parents dropped me off and Auntie Suzy called me into the kitchen where Michael was sitting down eating dried cereal with his fingers. She pointed at me and said, "Look Michael, Sariah," and she formed a shape with her hand that looked like a fist. That shape is the letter "s" in sign language. She also moved her hand down her hair to represent my long hair. That day my signed name became "Sariah with long hair." Auntie Suzy created a signed name for everybody in the family so Michael would know and be able to talk to them. When Auntie Suzy taught Michael a sign for me that day, I felt special. I was intrigued and wanted to learn more.

Later on, I realized that Michael really wasn't so different. We talked all the time and laughed about the craziest things. I honestly don't even know anybody who laughs more than Michael. I even remember going to Grandma's house on the weekends and having a butt race with Michael. We would go down the stairs on our butts really fast. Auntie didn't like us doing that. Sometimes, Auntie Suzy would tell me to help him practice going up and down the steps appropriately. She would say, "We can't teach him to be lazy." But we were kids, and it was so much fun.

We had to take things slow with Michael, and at times he would throw his little tantrums. But Michael knew when he acted up. Michael loves ice cream and, when he acts up, he does not get ice cream after dinner.

One summer, Auntie Suzy started a summer camp for Michael because she couldn't find one to put him in. She had the older cousins as tutors and the younger cousins as students, including Michael. She asked me to help her and be a tutor. Auntie Suzy prepared the lessons for us and we taught our little cousins. I was assigned as Michael's tutor. We had reading, writing, sign language, lunch and math. We went to the pool, movies and played games. We did our lessons in the morning and played in the afternoon. Michael was a goof-ball and played around, but instantly we got along and he would listen to me, so I became his tutor.

One day I was teaching him a new lesson about a clown, and Auntie Suzy taught everyone the sign for clown or someone who is silly. I gave the class an example of a clown and pretended to trip over my own two feet and Michael laughed hysterically and really couldn't stop. Ever since then, the word "silly" has kind of stuck with me. Every time he sees me now, he calls me silly. That summer I really worked with Michael and the other kids so well, I told my mother I wanted to be an occupational therapist one day.

At a young age, Michael taught me to appreciate the little things I do have and sometimes take for granted. He's the reason I'm more patient, more courteous, good-hearted, and considerate of others today. I learned to work so well with kids that I volunteered during my junior and senior year of high school in schools for disabled kids that were hard of hearing and/or blind. Today, I no longer look at disabled people as different or weird but more as special, because really and truly -- without realizing it -- Michael played a significant role in the character I have today. I no longer want to be an occupational therapist, but I have never stopped helping or giving a hand wherever it is needed.

Chapter 25

My Relationship with Michael

By Gilbert Franklin

We can say that we are fortunate to have Michael Augustin in our lives. There is much we can learn from him as an individual with limited mobility. My relationship with Michael as my nephew and the greeting that I receive from him does not change, even after not seeing him for period of time. He has continually showed me agape love every single time we meet.

Often time, people look at Michael and see his disability, not the person. He is a smart young man. Michael's inability to speak is manifested in different ways to those he loves. He demands your attention when you are in his presence and, in return, he expresses his love and appreciation for taking the time to acknowledge him.

Sometimes our conversations would start regarding mom's cooking, and of course he would compliment mom's cooking when she was around. We talk about school and his behavior. He gets this look on his face when we start to talk about his behavior -- he brings his head down and stares at the ground. He is physically disabled; however, mentally he seems to understand when I talk to him. I feel that in the right environment, Michael has the capability of learning a lot.

One summer Suzy started a summer camp with Michael, my daughters Chloe and Sabelle, and his cousin Bianca. That summer the children learned and experienced a lot working with Suzy and Michael.

Michael's aggression sometimes comes from his frustration at trying to communicate and not being understood. I remember one day Michael was trying to tell me something and I didn't understand. He urinated on himself and I proceeded to help clean him up. When I bent down to remove his pants, he smacked me so hard on the back of my head that I saw stars.

We can't talk about Michael's achievements without talking about Suzy's patience and understanding towards him. He looks lost when Suzy is not around. One day I stopped by the house to see Michael while his mom went on a weekend getaway. When I walked into the house, I didn't get my customary greeting with a high five. I could tell something was wrong. He seemed very upset. I asked his grandma what had happened. She said that Suzy went away for the weekend and he was not happy with her going away. That day when Suzy called to talk to him over phone, he refused to pick up the phone and listen or talk to her. I started to explain to him that sometimes his mom needed to get away in order to get recharge again so she could better help him. He obviously did not agree with my logic of the situation; or he was just too upset to listen.

Michael's mom thinks he's a jokester. We often joke about the amount of girlfriends that he has (he's joking, of course). When we talk about girls, he says that he is going to marry a normal girl, but his children will be disabled. The boy that I know will one day be a wonderful man, even with his physical disabilities. The day he realizes his capacity to achieve, the sky is the limit. Michael Augustin, I LOVE YOU.

Endnotes

Kingsley, E. P, (1987). Welcome to Holland. Retrieved from www.ourkids.org/Archives/Holland.html

Keller, H. Helen Keller Quotes. Author of Story of My Life. (1990).
Retrieved from www.goodreaders.com/author/quotes/7275. Helen_Keller

Bombeck, E. Some mothers are chosen very carefully. Retrieved from www.wordsfromwillow.blogspot.com

Michael & Tina
2004

Brittany & Michael
Christmas 2008

Michael (Age 5) & Chloe (Age 3)

Michael's 6th Birthday

Michael (Age 5) & Sariah (Age 8)

Michael
Halloween 1998

St. Augustine, FL
2000

Having fun at the pool with cousins

148

My praying grandma, Cledilia Jean,
with Michael & Brittany

Cruising with Family
(L-R) Brittany, Me, Jean & Michael

(L-R) Michael, Barbara, Steven, Tina,
Sepphira, Brittany, Chris & Jason

(L-R) Michael, Grandpa Ellie Paul & Grandma Rose

(L-R) Me, Grandpa Lucien, Brittany, Sapphira & Grandma Odette

Michael & Daddy

Me, Michael & Auntie Marianne
On our way to Animal Kingdom in Disney

Me, Michael & Auntie Maggie

Michael at Horse Therapy

Cousin Jason, Barbara & Michael

Uncle Ronald, Auntie Maggie & Christopher

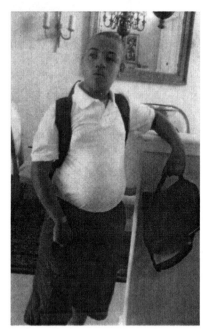

First Day of Middle School
12 years

Michael

Augustin

CPSIA information can be obtained at www.ICGtesting.com
Printed in the USA
LVOW11s1353161113

361561LV00003B/4/P

9 781624 193200